This book belongs to:

DLee was in class one day,
but things were just not going her way.

Lots of things kept going wrong.
First, Ms. Mayo forgot to say her name
during the morning circle song.

Second, when in art, DLee's friend Jolie drew on her rainbow colored heart.

Third, when in gym
and passing her friend Priscilla the ball,
DLee's friend Hiro ran into her
and made her fall!

4

Fourth, when DLee went to grab Ms. Mayo's new alphabet book, she saw her friend Maddox had ripped the pages before she even got to look.

DLee was mad!
DLee was sad!
She did not know
how to deal.
Because she did not
know what to feel.

She was not
having a good day.
Why did it have
to be this way?

6

DLee started to dwell.
Then she started to yell.

7

8

DLee was mad!
DLee was sad!
She did not know
how to deal.
Because she did not
know what to feel.

She was not
having a good day.
Why did it have
to be this way?

Then DLee found a stick.
And she started to kick.

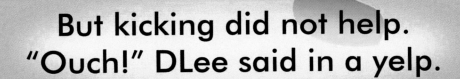

But kicking did not help.
"Ouch!" DLee said in a yelp.

DLee was mad!
DLee was sad!
She did not know
how to deal.
Because she did not
know what to feel.

She was not
having a good day.
Why did it have
to be this way?

12

So DLee started to cry.
But Ms. Mayo came over
with tissue to dry each eye.
"There! There! DLee!
No need to fear.
Your teacher,
Ms. Mayo is here.
Talk to me. Tell me
what is wrong, DLee."

13

DLee told Ms. Mayo
about her day.
And Ms. Mayo assured
her that those feelings
were normal and
it would be okay.
"Even if you start
to have a bad day,
it does not have
to stay that way."

14

"I know! Let us try to think of something fun to do.
I will think of something
but I want you to think too!"

15

"I have an idea. Let us sing your favorite song."
So as Ms. Mayo started to sing,
DLee smiled and sang along.

Then it was DLee's turn
to say what she wanted to do.
She was excited because she was able
to think of something fun too!

17

"I know! Let us hop!"
So the two grabbed hands and began to pop.
They hopped and bopped
until they dropped!

18

When they finished,
DLee was no longer mad.
DLee was no longer sad.
With Ms. Mayo's help,
DLee dealt with what she felt.

DLee was not having a bad day.
It did not have to be that way.
After finding some exciting things to play,
DLee was happy again and
ready to enjoy the rest of her day.

20

If you liked this book, check out DLee in:

www.dleesworld.com

Made in the USA
Middletown, DE
23 April 2021